Cell Phone Timeline

ca. 50,000–20,000 BCE

Digits: People's fingers are probably the first tools for calculation.

1843

English inventor Michael Faraday investigates whether empty space can conduct electricity.

1895

Italian inventor Guglielmo Marconi sends the first message using radio waves.

ca. 1492

Leonardo da Vinci designs the first mechanical calculator.

ca. 724 CE

Chinese engineer Liang Lingzan builds the first clock that ticks.

1834

English engineer Charles Babbage designs his Analytical Engine, the world's first computer.

1876

The world's first telephone is invented by Alexander Graham Bell.

1921

Detroit police install mobile radios in cars.

1992

The first text message is sent to a mobile phone by English engineer Neil Papworth.

1947

Scientists at Bell Labs devise the first cellular telephone system.

1997

French innovator Philippe Kahn sends the first photo taken by a mobile phone.

2007

The first phone with multi-touch technology is released—a genuine mobile computer.

1983

The first mobile phone, the DynaTAC, goes on sale. It costs $4,000.

1993

The world's first smart phone, the Simon, features a touch screen, e-mail, and a sketch pad.

1999

The first phones with an MP3 music player go on sale.

2008

The first app store is launched. By 2011, 15 billion apps have been downloaded.

Where Did Your Phone Come From?

Cell phones depend on rare materials from all over the globe.
This map shows just a few of the places involved in phone production.
Your phone may have come from all of these countries, and more.

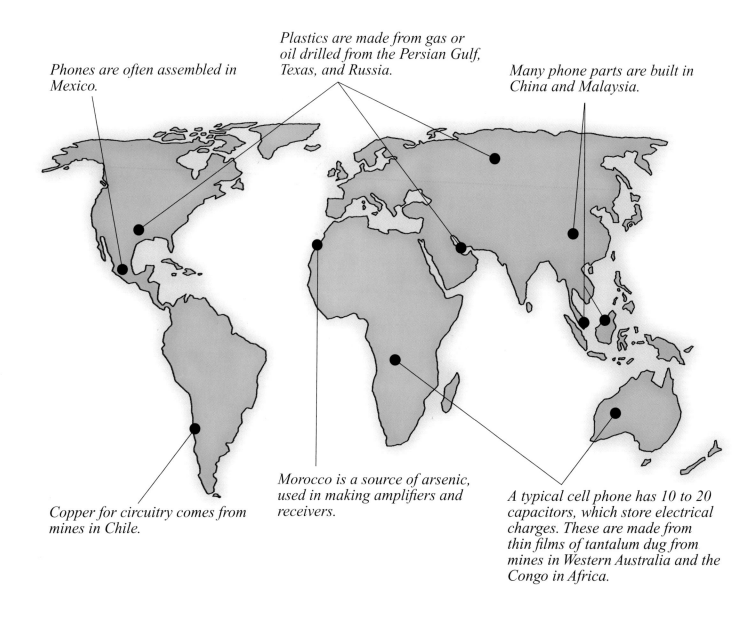

Phones are often assembled in Mexico.

Plastics are made from gas or oil drilled from the Persian Gulf, Texas, and Russia.

Many phone parts are built in China and Malaysia.

Copper for circuitry comes from mines in Chile.

Morocco is a source of arsenic, used in making amplifiers and receivers.

A typical cell phone has 10 to 20 capacitors, which store electrical charges. These are made from thin films of tantalum dug from mines in Western Australia and the Congo in Africa.

Author:

Jim Pipe studied ancient and modern history at Oxford University and spent 10 years in publishing before becoming a full-time writer. He has written numerous nonfiction books for children, many on historical subjects. He lives in Dublin, Ireland, with his wife and sons.

Artist:

Rory Walker is an artist and illustrator from deepest, darkest Snowdonia, Wales. He's created artwork for several hundred books and takes great delight in using a traditional pen and bottle of ink to create his images.

Series creator:

David Salariya was born in Dundee, Scotland. He has illustrated a wide range of books and has created and designed many new series for publishers in the UK and overseas. David established The Salariya Book Company in 1989. He lives in Brighton, England, with his wife, illustrator Shirley Willis, and their son, Jonathan.

Editors: **Caroline Coleman, Stephen Haynes**

Editorial Assistant: **Mark Williams**

PAPER FROM
SUSTAINABLE
FORESTS

© The Salariya Book Company Ltd MMXV

Published in Great Britain in 2015 by
The Salariya Book Company Ltd
25 Marlborough Place, Brighton BN1 1UB

ISBN-13: 978-0-531-21217-2 (lib. bdg.) 978-0-531-21308-7 (pbk.)

Published in 2015 in the United States
by Franklin Watts
An imprint of Scholastic Inc.
Published simultaneously in Canada.

A CIP catalog record for this book is available
from the Library of Congress.

Printed and bound in China.
Printed on paper from sustainable sources.

1 2 3 4 5 6 7 8 9 10 R 24 23 22 21 20 19 18 17 16 15

You Wouldn't Want to Live Without™
Cell Phones!

Written by
Jim Pipe

Illustrated by
Rory Walker

Created and designed by
David Salariya

Franklin Watts®
An Imprint of Scholastic Inc.
NEW YORK • TORONTO • LONDON • AUCKLAND • SYDNEY
MEXICO CITY • NEW DELHI • HONG KONG
DANBURY, CONNECTICUT

Contents

Introduction

Cell phones are such a part of our daily lives in the 21st century, it's hard to imagine our world without them. In just a few years, these minicomputers have transformed the way we live, work, and play, allowing us to do everything from shopping and banking online to downloading music, streaming videos, or catching up with our friends 24/7 using texts or instant messaging. Entire movie plots have centered around a cell phone. Now, picture your life without your cell phone. Terrifying thought, isn't it?

THERE'S NO END to what the latest smartphones can do, from reporting the weather to providing maps and travel directions. A United Nations study in 2013 revealed that out of the world's estimated 7 billion people, 6 billion have access to cell phones—while only 4.5 billion people have access to working toilets!

The Wonder Gadget

Arguably, the cell phone has changed the world more quickly than almost any other invention. It performs so many different functions that it has sent a whole bunch of other gadgets to the trash can. Weighing less than 3 ounces (85 grams), and small enough to fit into a shirt pocket, it goes everywhere we go. No wonder some 1.8 billion cell phones were sold in 2013. If you lined them up sideways, they would reach halfway to the moon! Now, imagine living 100 years ago or more, when there were no cell phones…

TICKTOCK. When Swiss clockmaker Jost Bürgi invented the minute hand in 1577, he kick-started the world's obsession with knowing the exact time. Pocket or "fob" watches became popular in the 1700s, and wristwatches arrived in the 1920s.

IF YOU'D TRIED to build a smartphone in the 19th century, it wouldn't have been very mobile!

Music

Camera

Phone

GPS

Clock

Games

Calculator

Flashlight

It'll never catch on!

GIVE ME A BELL. In 1876, Alexander Graham Bell yelled the famous words, "Mr. Watson—come here—I want to see you!" through the world's first telephone. By 1914, there were millions of landline phones across Europe and the United States.

SAY CHEESE! In 1826, it took 8 hours for Joseph Nicéphore Niépce to create the world's first photograph (left). By 1900, you could take good-quality snapshots using the Kodak Brownie, a simple $1 box camera that used a roll of film.

WANDERFUL. Even 100 years ago, there were still large unexplored areas in the world. These days, the Global Positioning System (GPS) allows a phone to calculate your position to within 50 feet (15 meters) almost anywhere on the planet.

MOBILE DISCO. In medieval times, minstrels went from castle to castle playing music and songs. Today, music apps can turn anyone into an instant DJ.

7

What, No Instant Messaging?

Allô? Cavalry? I want you to charge down the right flank. Yes, in 5 minutes. Merci!

f you sent a text to a friend and didn't hear back for a month, how would you feel? Well, before the invention of the telephone, the quickest way to keep in touch with other people was to write a letter. Chances were, after handing your letter to a courier who galloped off into the distance, you'd wait weeks for a reply. Frustrated Frenchman Renouard De Valayer tried to set up the first postal system in 1653, but his cunning plan was foiled when a rival dropped mice into his mailboxes to nibble all the letters. Even with the arrival of a modern postal system in the 1840s, it could take days for a letter to arrive.

IMAGINE how differently things might have worked out if Napoleon had had a cell phone at the Battle of Waterloo in 1815.

Air today, gone tomorrow, sir!

AIRMAIL. During World War I, the carrier pigeon Cher Ami carried messages to U.S. troops, despite losing a foot to enemy fire.

One hundred years ago, a trained Morse operator could send 40 to 50 words per minute. Can you text that fast?

AT A GALLOP. In the 1200s, the messengers of Mongol emperor Genghis Khan rode up to 185 miles (300 kilometers) in a single day. A network of 1,400 relay stations provided the riders with food and fresh horses.

RAIL MAIL (below left). In their day, stamps were as revolutionary as cell phones. The Penny Black, introduced in England in 1840, was the world's first postage stamp. Stamps were put into use to fund the postal service.

DASHES AND DOTS. Samuel Morse showed that messages could be sent along electric wires when he invented the electric telegraph (below) in 1835. A system of short and long taps—dots and dashes—stood for letters.

9

Riding the Airwaves

Today, it takes just a few taps on a touch screen to send a quick message via cell phone. In the past, fires and smoke signals were used to send messages quickly over long distances. Fastest of all were African drummers who sent signals at speeds of up to 100 mph (160 kph).

By 1848, the electric telegraph provided instant long-distance communication, and in 1895 Italian inventor Guglielmo Marconi sent the first message using radio waves. But there was a catch: Only a few hundred people could use the airwaves at a time without everyone listening in to each others' conversations. Can you imagine?

IN 1920s AMERICA, radios were used to catch gangsters smuggling alcohol. At first, patrolmen had to stop their cars and hook up to a telephone wire. But by 1928, officers in Detroit were using voice-based radio in their cars.

Alpha Bravo Charlie, my dog could drive better than that.

He says his arms are getting sore!

SEMAPHORE is a system of sending messages using a pair of handheld flags or paddles. It was often used by ships in the 1800s and is still used for emergency communication today.

WALKIE-TALKIE. This 35-pound (15-kilogram) radio invented during World War II allowed soldiers to communicate on the battlefield. It had a push-to-talk (PTT) system where you pushed the button to speak, then let it go to hear the sound from other radios.

You Can Do It!

Citizens Band, or CB radio, is a two-way radio network where everyone can hear everyone else. It became popular in the 1970s, especially with truck drivers, who had nicknames (or "handles") like River Rat and Rubber Duck. What would your handle be?

CAR PHONES. Radiophones appeared in 1946. They were big enough to fill the trunk of a car! And even in a big city like New York, there were just 12 radio channels.

PRANK CALLS. In mid-1950s Britain, only the Duke of Edinburgh (the Queen's husband) was allowed to have a private radiophone. He put it to good use—doing funny voices to amuse his children.

Cells

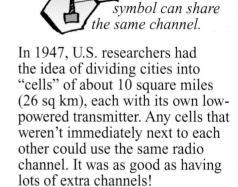

Cells with this symbol can share the same channel.

In 1947, U.S. researchers had the idea of dividing cities into "cells" of about 10 square miles (26 sq km), each with its own low-powered transmitter. Any cells that weren't immediately next to each other could use the same radio channel. It was as good as having lots of extra channels!

Beware the Brick!

Though dividing cities into cells was a big step toward modern cellular phones, it was another 25 years before technology made them a reality. It also took batteries light enough to make the phones portable, microchips to identify individual phones, and the right software to enable phones to maintain a signal when moving from cell to cell. Even when all of this was put together, no one guessed in the 1980s that the mobile phone was going to be the ultimate gadget of the early 21st century. Would you want to carry around a giant brick?

CALL ME BRICK. In 1983, the DynaTAC was the first cell phone to go on sale in the United States. Nicknamed the brick, it was huge because it held such a large battery. Earlier phones needed a whole briefcase to carry the battery.

AND THE WINNER IS…On April 3, 1973, inventor Martin Cooper made a call on an early version of the "brick." He called his rival to let him know he'd won the race to develop the first handheld device. His phone weighed 2.5 pounds (1.1 kg). It had a single-line, text-only LED screen, and a battery life of 20 minutes.

Wow! He must be really important.

NOT-SO-SIMPLE SIMON. The world's first smartphone, the Simon, appeared in 1993. It came with e-mail, a calendar, a diary, an address book, a calculator, and a sketch pad (left). It had one of the first touch-screen displays as well as predictive typing that guessed the characters as you typed.

How It Works

To use a cell phone, you have to be within range of an antenna (aerial) that can transmit the signal to other antennas. Many of these are cleverly disguised—as trees or cacti, for example—so they don't spoil the view.

TXT MSG. The first text was sent from a computer to a cell phone in 1992. English programmer Neil Papworth wished a friend "Merry Christmas." By 2013, people worldwide would be sending 9 trillion text messages a year.

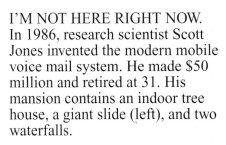

I'M NOT HERE RIGHT NOW. In 1986, research scientist Scott Jones invented the modern mobile voice mail system. He made $50 million and retired at 31. His mansion contains an indoor tree house, a giant slide (left), and two waterfalls.

HAPPY SNAP. On June 11, 1997, French engineer Philippe Kahn sent the first photo taken by a cell phone—of his newborn baby, Sophie.

Mini-Marvels

THINKING ENGINE. Way back in 1834, English inventor Charles Babbage came up with the idea of an arithmetic processor that calculated numbers and stored the results. Mathematician Ada Lovelace wrote the first computer program for it. Sadly, Babbage ran out of money and his machine was never built.

AS RECENTLY AS THE 1980s, a computer carrying out the same functions as a cell phone would have filled an entire floor of an office building.

Technology generally gets smaller and smaller, but it was 1989 before a cell phone was built that could fit in a shirt pocket. Phones have become a lot cheaper, too: The first ones cost as much as a small car. Just how did phones make the quantum leap from the cumbersome "bricks" of the 1970s to today's tiny titans? Improvements in batteries played an important role, but a whole range of other clever ideas—some a lot older than you might think—make modern smartphones the mini-marvels they are.

What's in Your Phone?

Keyboard
LCD display
Speaker
Microphone
Antenna
Circuit board
Battery

The circuit board contains the processor, the "brains" of your cell phone.

POWER PACK. The first known battery may have been built by an ancient Persian, who placed an iron rod inside a copper cylinder and sealed both of these inside a jar of acidic grape or lemon juice. Some 2,000 years later, modern batteries work in much the same way, though the materials are very different.

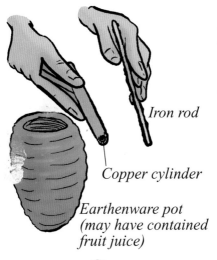

Iron rod

Copper cylinder

Earthenware pot (may have contained fruit juice)

SKINNY CHIPS. In 1958, American Jack Kilby developed the first integrated circuit, a set of electronic circuits on a small plate (or "chip"). The next year, Robert Noyce independently came up with an integrated circuit made out of silicon. Their discoveries launched the computer revolution of the next 50 years. Modern chips the size of a fingernail can contain several billion transistors and other electronic components.

THE LIQUID CRYSTAL DISPLAY (LCD) screen makes games, videos, address books, and text messaging possible. The curious properties of liquid crystals were first spotted by Austrian botanist Friedrich Reinitzer in the 1880s, but LCDs first appeared on watches and calculators nearly 100 years later, in the 1970s.

Forgotten Your Memory?

Phones also got a lot smarter. By 2007, they were full-blown minicomputers, allowing us to organize everything from writing e-mails to paying bills or looking for jobs. Can't remember something? Just type your query into a search engine and there's the answer. No wonder cell phones are banned from classrooms, exams, and quizzes. But, should you ever lose your phone (the horror!), here are a few old-fashioned tricks to help jog your memory.

Remember, Remember...

SCRIBBLERS. For the last 5,000 years, people have been making marks on stone, clay, and paper to record their thoughts. The ancient Egyptians loved making lists, whether writing down how many soldiers were in the army, or painting spells onto tomb walls to help guide a dead soul to the afterlife.

TO REMEMBER the number of days in each month, clench your fists. Each knuckle represents a long month (31 days), while the dips in between stand for the shorter months.

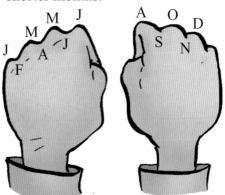

THANKS, GRANNY! Simple memory tricks are called mnemonics. The phrase "Rinse Out Your Granny's Boots In Vinegar," for example, lists the colors of the rainbow in order.

FEATS OF MEMORY. Before tales were written down, storytellers could make their stories last for hours by linking together smaller phrases they had memorized. In recent years, memorizing things has become a sport.

Hark to my tale...

Lovely work. But don't you spell 🦅 with a ☥?

(Well, some people can.) A Grand Master of Memory is someone who can memorize: (1) 1,000 random digits in an hour (2) the order of ten decks of cards in an hour (3) the order of one deck of cards in under two minutes. In January 2014, there were just 149 Grand Masters of Memory in the world.

SHORTHAND. In the 1660s, English civil servant Samuel Pepys wrote his diary in shorthand to keep it secret. A faster system of writing words in symbols and abbreviations was developed by Sir Isaac Pitman in 1837 and is still used today.

SONGLINES. Aboriginal peoples navigated their way across the vast deserts of the Australian wilderness by remembering songs that described the location of hills, water holes, and other natural landmarks. Do some songs make you think of particular times and places in your life?

17

Cell Phone Fun

With smartphones came multi-touch screens and instant access to a world of online entertainment. Today, American and European teenagers typically use mobile phones for around 2 hours each day. But only 12 minutes are used for making calls—the rest of the time is spent browsing the Internet, watching movies, listening to music, or playing games. Even toddlers got hooked in 2010, when the first successful tablet was launched, its book-sized screen allowing little fingers to join the party. So how did people entertain themselves before smartphones?

MASS KARAOKE. In the early 1900s, movie audiences enjoyed their own "interactive" media, including the Illustrated Song, where crowds sang along to lyrics projected onto the screen.

Oh, my darling,

Screech

Wail

MUSIC ON THE MOVE. In the 1950s, some cars were fitted with record players in the dashboard. Not much use on a bumpy road!

OLD-FASHIONED FUN. Around 2,000 years ago, the Romans enjoyed playing board games, going to the theater, or watching gladiators fight each other. On a cell phone, you can play games, watch movies, or fight digital battles with other players online—not so different, perhaps.

You Can Do It!

See how many smartphone gestures you know, from three-finger swipes to pinch-to-zoom. In the future, phones may also recognize hand gestures and facial expressions.

Grid

Controller (circuit board)

Screen

IN CONTROL. Fingers have always been great creative tools, whether making pots from clay, holding a pencil, or playing an instrument. But the touch screen brings a new level of control.

Behind a layer of tough glass is an invisible grid of fine electrical wires. When your finger swipes the screen, it creates an electrical disturbance that tells the computer inside your phone what to do.

SAME OLD STORY? Improvements in printing in the 1440s led to an information revolution. Before then, books had to be painstakingly written out by hand. The Internet, and e-readers, created a similar revolution. But, however you read it, a good story is a good story!

19

Phone a Friend!

Before cell phones, if you heard a voice behind you saying "Hello!" you'd turn around to see if it was a friend. These days, that voice is far more likely to be someone chatting on a cell phone. For many people, cell phones offer a way to keep in touch with their friends and family—all the time. Social networks allow us to share thoughts, pictures, and videos. Businesses, too, rely on them to find out what their customers want. But all that texting, e-mailing, and posting can seem like a full-time job! Could you survive without your social network? Let's see how people managed in the past.

LIKE? There have always been social networks. Rock art found in Russia and Sweden suggests that Bronze Age tribes communicated by leaving marks on rocks. These sites may have given different groups an opportunity to build up knowledge and share tips about hunting and other survival skills.

Do you think they want to unfriend us?

I fear there may be war with the Dutch again.

DAILY PERK. In the 1600s, gentlemen would visit their favorite coffeehouses several times a day to check for new mail and catch up on the news. Some coffeehouses specialized in chats about particular topics, such as science, literature, or trade.

You have no new messages.

VOICE MAIL. When Thomas Edison invented the gramophone in 1877, he hoped it would be used for recording telephone calls or dictating letters. In 1898, Danish inventor Valdemar Poulsen created the first magnetic machine for recording calls (left). It worked similarly to videotapes and computer drives.

IN 2010, Melissa Thompson smashed the record for the fastest text ever: 25.94 seconds to type a 160-character phrase.

FACE TIME. In the 1990s, the technology existed for video phones, but people usually preferred to keep their facial expressions hidden while talking on the phone. Video calls are becoming more and more popular—though it's probably best to avoid them first thing in the morning!

Did you sleep well?

SHORT & TWEET. German engineer Friedhelm Hillebrand came up with the 160-character size limit for text messages by typing random questions such as "What am I doing with my life?" and counting the characters. The first tweet was sent on March 21, 2006; by the end of 2013, more than 180 billion tweets had gone out worldwide.

21

101 Uses for a Cell Phone

What would you miss most if you lost your phone? Cell phones are used in ways their inventors never expected. Soldiers call home from the battlefield, African fishermen use them to find out the latest fish prices, and phones remind parents about lifesaving vaccination appointments for their children. In 2000, jokes spread around the Philippines by mobile phone (100 million texts a day!) helped to bring down the government. And, because cell phones have largely replaced landlines, they are a powerful way to send out warning messages. In the desert country of Oman, the government sends out texts to warn citizens about dangerous flash floods.

Hi, Dad!

WAR AND PEACE. While soldiers are already using cell phones to call home, the next generation of military phones will feature extra security features, waterproof cases for use underwater, and low-light screens that cannot be detected at night.

Cell phone users in the Philippines can often text equally fast with either hand. Using different fingers or swapping hands is also a good way to rest sore fingers and thumbs!

IN 2010, Haiti was hit with a devastating earthquake. Immediately afterward, studies mapped cell phone traffic there to see where people went after the disaster. Around 10 months later, this information was a big help to relief agencies coping with an outbreak of the deadly disease cholera.

CHEAP CALLS. Even in the poorest parts of Africa, many people have access to cell phones. In West Africa, at roadsides, "umbrella ladies" set up their cell phone business with a chair, a phone, and shade from the sun. Some users cut costs by "flashing"—letting the phone ring once and then hanging up. Friends use these missed calls as a code.

HEALTH. Medical devices are being developed that can be linked to a cell phone to diagnose illnesses such as pneumonia, which kills 2 million people a year. New software will use a cell phone's computing power to work out what medicine, and how much, should be given to patients.

It says you're faking it.

Cell Phones to the Rescue!

Has your cell phone ever helped someone find you in a busy shopping mall? Cell phones also work well in the wild. Thanks to the Global Positioning System (GPS), even a faint signal can be used by rescue teams to pinpoint people lost in remote areas. In 2011, a skier trapped on a mountain in Italy phoned her father 800 miles (1,300 km) away in England. He called the Italian emergency services, and his daughter and her friend were saved.

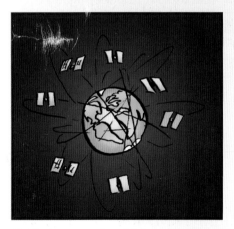

GPS. A network of 24 satellites orbiting 12,000 miles (19,000 km) above Earth allows a cell phone to figure out your position to within 50 feet (15 m), almost anywhere on the planet. The satellites make two complete orbits of Earth in less than 24 hours.

SOME APPS can turn a cell phone into a rescue beacon. Even when you don't have a standard phone signal, they connect with a low-orbiting satellite system. The apps also map your route online, so you can be found in an emergency.

Just look at this, Carruthers!

Top Tip

Are you always losing your cell phone? Inventors are now working on the idea of keeping your SIM card safe by inserting it into your forearm. For many people, the data stored on their SIM card is more precious than the phone itself.

SHINE A LIGHT. Don't forget, you can also use your cell phone as a flashlight (though it will wear the battery down quickly). Apps have been developed that turn the phone into a Morse code transmitter, too.

HELP! In the past, flares, whistles, drums, smoke signals, and fire beacons were used to warn of danger. Cell phones make the job a lot faster. In some parts of the United States, you can text the police instead of dialing 911.

SAFE AND SOUND. Cell phones come in handy when you want to let others know you've reached your destination safely. In May 2013, British climber Daniel Hughes made history by making the first live video call from the top of the world's highest peak, Mount Everest, 29,029 feet (8,848 m) above sea level.

South coast of England, 1588: Lighting a beacon to warn of the approach of the Spanish Armada.

Bad Habits

Do you know any cell phone addicts? One in three teens sends more than 100 text messages a day—or 3,000 texts a month—and two out of three teenagers sleep with their mobile phones close to them. Many people can't help checking their phones first thing in the morning and last thing at night, and their virtual friends are more important than the person sitting in front of them. On trains and buses, passengers sit silently glued to their phones, each in their own bubble. In fact, many teenagers say they would rather live without chocolate and TV than be without their phone!

PHONE SNIFFERS. Cell phones have been banned in all sorts of places, from theaters and movie theaters to schools and prisons. Cell phones have been smuggled into prisons inside books, milk cartons, and shoes. However, cell phones have a unique scent, and special dogs have been trained to sniff them out!

OMG! It has always been good to keep in touch, whether passing along the latest joke or gossip, or sharing your feelings. Four thousand years ago, a lovestruck man in ancient Babylon wrote this message to his sweetheart—not so different from a text today!

To Bibea: Tell me how you are. I went to Babylon but I did not see you. I was really disappointed. Tell me why you are leaving, to cheer me up. For my sake keep well always. Gimil.

Fetch!

Top tip

When it comes to your night-time routine, avoid looking at your phone. The blue-white light given off by a cell phone can fool your body into thinking it's daytime, keeping you awake.

WARNING: Though there's no solid proof that cell phones aren't safe to use, you should avoid keeping them under your pillow at night.

Phone Phobias

Do any of your friends suffer from the following?

• **Telephonobia:** The fear of making or receiving phone calls.

• **Ringxiety:** You hear your phone ringing, even when it's not.

• **Nomophobia** (no-mobile-phone phobia): Feeling anxious when you don't have your cell phone on you or can't get a signal.

• **Frigensophobia:** The fear that using your cell phone is damaging your brain.

Smart Devices, Smart Users?

Thanks to cell phones, we now take for granted things that just a few decades ago only happened in science fiction: texting, video chat, instant driving directions, and being able to reach anyone, anywhere, anytime. But beware, these clever gadgets are only as smart as their users! In 2013, a woman distracted by a text message drove straight into a lake in Maryland. Luckily she escaped unhurt from the sinking car, but it shows just why driving while texting or talking on a cell phone has been banned in many countries around the world. Texting while driving makes a driver 23 times more likely to crash—and kills 11 teenagers each day.

ONE IN TEN SMARTPHONE OWNERS have given their handsets a watery grave by dropping them into a toilet. Other mishaps include a dead man's cell phone that started ringing from inside the coffin, and the woman who claimed a seagull had swooped down and flown off with hers!

POCKET-DIALING. Police officers in Daytona Beach, Florida, in 2010 were able to prevent a car burglary after one of the thieves "pocket-dialed"—he sat on his phone, triggering a 911 call to the police.

DOG PHONES. In 2007, a cell phone with built-in GPS was designed especially for dogs. This allowed the owners to track their dog's movements, and sent an alert if they strayed beyond a certain point. It didn't take off, despite claiming to be waterproof.

Look, there's an app for finding bones.

HIGHLY MOBILE. A pyrotechnician (fireworks expert) was setting up a show as part of the National Fireworks Championships in Plymouth, England. Later, he realized he had accidentally fired his phone 3,000 feet (900 m) into the air as part of the display!

29

Glossary

Antenna A device for sending or receiving radio signals. Most smartphones have internal antennas, but older phones had antennas sticking out of them. Tall antennas mounted on a tower or mast are used to create cellular networks (see **cell**, below).

App Short for *application*, a software program for cell phones and tablet computers.

Band A particular range of radio frequencies, for example, those used by wireless companies to provide a cell phone signal.

Cell The area covered by a cell phone mast, or tower antenna. Each tower overlaps with the coverage of nearby towers, so your phone does not stop working as you move from one cell to another. A series of overlapping cells is called a cellular network.

GPS Short for Global Positioning System, a network of satellites that pinpoints the exact location of people and objects. If you dial an emergency number, GPS allows operators to figure out where you are.

Instant messaging Internet-based "chat" software that allows people to send quick text messages to each other. It shows you at a glance which of your friends is available for a chat.

Landline A standard, non-wireless telephone connection.

Liquid crystal display (LCD) A common type of screen display made up of tiny squares called pixels. LCD displays are generally easy to read and use relatively little energy.

Microchip A set of electronic circuits on one small plate (or "chip"), usually made out of silicon.

Mobile phone Another name for a cellular or wireless phone.

NiCad battery A rechargeable battery with key parts made out of nickel and cadmium.

Numeric keypad A standard telephone keypad, with four rows of three keys each. The top row consists of 1, 2, and 3; the last row usually has *, 0, and #.

Processor The "brain" of a cell phone (or any other kind of computer). It handles the instructions of software apps. A faster processor allows apps to run faster. Also called a central processing unit (CPU).

SIM card Short for "subscriber identity module"—a plastic card containing a microchip that stores the information you need to use your phone.

Smartphone A cell phone that is more like a minicomputer and can run many different kinds of software. Smartphones often have larger displays and more powerful processors than older, simpler phones.

Software All the programs that enable a computer to function—as opposed to hardware, which is the computer (or other electronic device) itself.

Telegraph A 19th-century system for sending messages over long distances along a wire.

Text messaging Software that allows short text messages to be sent and received on a cell phone. Also called SMS (Short Message Service).

Touch screen A screen on a cell phone that, when tapped, activates a button or a feature displayed at that point on the screen.

Voice mail A digital answering machine provided by a phone network that stores a call made when the person being called is unavailable. It usually plays a greeting message and records the voice message from the caller.

Walkie-talkie A two-way radio that allows you to speak to all other users in range, by pushing a "talk" button.

Wireless Able to send information without using wires. For example, a cell phone uses radio waves instead of wires to send messages and data.

Index

Cell Phone Talk

The growth of text messaging in the 1990s saw the creation of a whole new way of writing, known as "textese" or "txt speak." Twenty years ago, most mobile phones had numeric keypads where you had to tap a number key several times to get the right letter. With hundreds of millions of people texting every day, all sorts of abbreviations were developed to save time. Here are some popular ones; do you know any others?

2NITE Tonight
A3 Anytime, anyplace, anywhere
BFF Best friends forever
BRB Be right back
CAAC Cool as a cucumber
CUL8R See you later
G2G Got to go
GR8 Great
HMU Hit me up (Contact me)
ICWUM I see what you mean
JK Just kidding
LOL Laugh out loud

MEGO My eyes glaze over (How boring!)
NVM Never mind
ROFL Rolling on floor, laughing
SFSG So far, so good
SUP What's up?
TTYL Talk to you later
WBU What about you?

Did You Know?

- According to one scientific study, cell phones have 18 times more bacteria on them than the handle of a toilet.

- In Japan, most cell phones are made waterproof because so many people, especially teenagers, use them in the shower.

- Scientists in a UK laboratory have found a way of charging cell phones using chemical reactions powered by human urine.

- Alexander Graham Bell recommended "Ahoy!" as the telephone greeting (as used on ships), but fellow inventor Thomas Edison saved the world from speaking forever like a pirate by suggesting "Hello" instead.

- Chances are you've received a phantom call on your cell phone, usually from a phone in someone's pocket or bag. For the emergency services, it's a serious problem. In the early 2000s the National Emergency Number Association revealed that phantom calls were responsible for 70 percent of 911 calls in some areas.

- In 1860, Johann Philipp Reis built the first modern telephone using a cork, a knitting needle, a sausage skin, and a piece of platinum. The scientists he showed it to laughed at it. However, Reis coined the word *telephone*, still used by billions of people today.

- There is a museum dedicated to mobile phones in Dublin, Ireland.

Top New Phone Habits

Cell phones have changed the way we behave in all sorts of unexpected ways. Have you ever done any of the following? If you haven't, you probably will—they are all increasingly common.

- If your cell phone has a two-way camera, point it at your face. Then use it as a high-tech mirror to do your makeup or brush your hair!

- Don't bother knocking or using doorbells anymore. Just call from your phone when you are standing outside the door.

- Got something stuck in your teeth? Ask a friend to take a closer look, using the flashlight on their phone.

- If you love your new haircut, get a friend to take pictures of you from all sides so you can show it to the hairdresser the next time you go.

- Feeling stressed? Some phone apps help by letting you pop sheets of digital bubble wrap.

- If you can't find your glasses, looking through a phone camera can help you see more clearly.

- In a recent survey in the United States, 4 out of 10 people admitted that when they met a friend on the street they sometimes looked at their phone to avoid starting a conversation. A similar number did a quick Internet search to help them follow a conversation.

- Ringtones can be very irritating. But to moms who want to calm a crying baby, a ringing phone is an instant musical toy!

- Take pictures of your friends holding the things you've lent them, so you'll remember to ask for them back.